WILD BEARS!

GRIZZLY BEAR

By Jason and Jody Stone
Photographs by Tom and Pat Leeson

BLACKBIRCH PRESS, INC.

WOODBRIDGE, CONNECTICUT

Published by Blackbirch Press, Inc.
260 Amity Road
Woodbridge, CT 06525

Email: staff@blackbirch.com
Web site: www.blackbirch.com

Printed in the United States

10 9 8 7 6 5 4 3 2 1

All photographs ©Tom and Pat Leeson.

Library of Congress Cataloging-in-Publication Data
Stone, Jason.
Grizzly bear/ by Jason and Jody Stone.
    p. cm. — (Wild bears!)
    Summary: Describes the physical appearance, habits, hunting and mating behaviors, family life, and life cycle of the grizzly bear.
    ISBN 1-56711-342-7 (hardcover : alk. paper)
    1. Grizzly bear—Juvenile literature. [1. Grizzly bear. 2. Bears.] I. Stone, Jody, 1975— II. Title. III. Series.
QL737.C27 SL68 2000
599.784—dc21
                                        00-009039

Contents

Introduction

Out of all the species of bears in the world, grizzly bears are found in the most locations. Scientists believe that there are about 125,000 to 150,000 grizzlies living in the wild. Most of these bears live in parts of North America, Asia, and Europe.

In North America, grizzly bears inhabit the mountains, meadows, and beaches of Canada, Alaska, and a few areas in Idaho, Montana, and Wyoming.

Where Grizzlies Are Most Common

Arctic Ocean

Europe

Asia

North America

Atlantic Ocean

Pacific Ocean

Africa

Pacific Ocean

South America

Indian Ocean

Australia

KEY
■ Grizzly territory

But since the 1800s, the North American grizzly bear population has been cut in half. Today, only about 45,000 grizzlies can be found there.

Grizzlies, also known as brown bears, are not the only bear species that lives in North America. Polar bears live in the Arctic much farther north than the grizzly's range. While black bears and grizzly bears often share the same ranges, they each use a different habitat. Black bears like to stay in the forest while grizzly bears prefer to feed in open areas, prairies, or alpine meadows.

In North America, grizzlies prefer to roam the open prairies or meadows near mountains.

The Grizzly Body

A grizzly bear has a large body, short legs, small ears, and a short tail.

Some male grizzly bears may weigh more than 1,000 pounds (454 kilograms), but most weigh between 300 to 400 pounds (136 to 181 kilograms). Males measure about 3.5 feet (1 meter) tall at the shoulder, and are about 7 feet (2 meters) long. Males are about twice as big as females.

Grizzly bears were named for the color of their fur. These bears are usually a brown or blond color, except for the tips of their hairs. Each tip is a light gray color. Because of this, their brown coats have a "grizzled" appearance. Grizzled means "gray haired."

Left: Standing upright, a male grizzly can be more than 7 feet (2 meters) tall.
Opposite: A hump in the shoulders and very long claws are two of a grizzly's unique physical traits.

Grizzly bear bodies look similar to black bear bodies. But besides the coloring, there are three features of a grizzly bear that distinguish it from a black bear. A grizzly has a noticeable hump above its shoulders, a dish-shaped face, and very long claws.

The large shoulder hump on a grizzly is actually a massive group of muscles that give the animal strength in its arms. The grizzly uses this strength—together with its long claws—to dig up roots and bulbs to eat. Particularly in the spring and early summer, a grizzly can tear up acres of sod in a day while it eats tender new shoots and roots.

Special Features

A grizzly bear has a very keen sense of smell. Grizzlies use their sense of smell to detect danger and to locate food. They can smell berries and rotting flesh from several miles away. Grizzly bears can even discover food buried under snow or soil!

Grizzlies will swim to capture fish.

The claws on a grizzly are 4 to 5 inches (10 to 12 centimeters) long—twice as long as black bear claws. Unlike the black bear, which uses its claws for tree climbing, grizzly bears mainly use their claws for digging. Finding ground squirrels and digging them out of their holes is a favorite grizzly trick. Grizzlies also use their claws to grasp objects—even things as small as berries, which they pick and eat in the fall.

Above and right: Grizzlies use their excellent sense of smell to locate food and detect danger.

Although bears prefer to use their noses to find food and identify their surroundings, a grizzly can also hear and see very well. Grizzlies can hear better than humans do. In fact, a grizzly can hear a human speak more than .25 miles (.40 kilometers) away!

Social Life

Most grizzly bears live alone. Because a grizzly needs to eat a lot of food, it will claim and protect an area with a good food source. Once a grizzly finds a territory, it will live, hunt, and raise its young there. This area is called a bear's home range. Grizzly bears remain in their own home ranges to avoid fighting with other bears. Occasionally, when an area has plenty of food, grizzlies will gather to feed. In Alaska and Canada, where salmon still survive in large numbers, grizzlies gather along rivers to catch fish.

Left: Where food is plentiful, grizzlies will share an area.
Opposite: When food is scarce, grizzlies will fight to defend their territory.

When bears are close together, they use body signals to communicate whether they will attack or tolerate another bear's presence. A bear that is threatened will usually lower its head, flatten its ears, and directly face the other bear. A grizzly that wants to fight may snort or growl at other bears.

Hibernation

Because it is hard to find food during the long winter, some bears have the amazing ability to hibernate (be inactive or in a resting state). A grizzly will hibernate for many months until spring returns (usually 5 to 7 months). Before they hibernate, grizzlies must spend most of their time eating to build up enough fat to survive so many months without food.

Long, cold winter months mean little food is available.

Before hibernation, a bear will eat and rest a great deal in order to prepare for the winter ahead.

In late fall, a grizzly must find a place to hibernate. Where trees grow at high elevations, grizzlies will often dig a den beneath tree roots or under a large rock. Sometimes they use a natural cave. When a bear goes into hibernation, its body temperature drops, and the bear survives on stored body fat.

The Food Supply

"Hungry as a bear" certainly describes the grizzly. To maintain its great size and strength, a grizzly is always searching for food. Because grizzlies eat both meat and plants, they are called omnivores. The season and the type of food available in a bear's home range determine its diet. Grizzly bears use meadows in their home range to find edible plants, such as berries, roots, and grass.

Below: Plants, berries, and roots are part of a grizzly's diet.
Opposite: Grizzlies are expert fishers and will even dig for clams on a beach (inset).

Some bears that live near streams and rivers in Western Canada and Alaska hunt for fish. In the summer and fall, when the salmon return to spawn (lay eggs), bears can reach into rivers with their mouths or claws to catch fish. Bears living on the coast even dig for clams at the beach!

Grizzlies will hunt for insects and small animals under rocks, inside logs, or inside rotting tree stumps.

In the spring, a grizzly often hunts for small animals because they are easy to catch. The grizzly's keen sense of smell also helps it to find animals that have died. Once a grizzly kills an animal, it will cover it with dirt and stay nearby until it is safe to eat. Grizzlies also hunt for insects and grubs by tearing apart old logs and tree stumps.

GRIZZLIES: THE BEAR FACTS

What makes grizzlies different from other bears? Here are some quick facts about the special qualities of these powerful animals.

Identifying a Grizzly:

There are four physical features that are unique to grizzly bears. They are:

1. **Muscle Hump**: A large hump of muscle between the shoulders provides super power to a grizzly's arms.
2. **"Dished" Face**: A grizzly has a hollow or "dished" area between the nose and eyes.
3. **Extra-Long Claws**: Grizzlies have longer claws than black bears.
4. **Dark Chest**: Many black bears have a light area on their chest. Grizzlies don't.

More About Grizzlies:

- The grizzly is the largest land carnivore in North America.
- In the fall, when a grizzly is trying to gain weight before hibernation, one bear can eat up to 200,000 berries in a single day.

- Grizzlies have an excellent sense of smell. Some bears can smell berries or animals from more than a mile away.
- When grizzlies stand on their hind feet, they're not getting ready to attack—they're just trying to get a better view and increase their ability to smell what's in the air.
- Grizzlies are incredibly fast for their size. Some bears weighing about 600 pounds (272 kg) can run as fast as a horse.

Protection Facts:

- Before Europeans arrived in what is today the United States, there were about 50,000 grizzlies in the wild. Today, scientists estimate that there are only 1,000 grizzlies in the lower 48 states.
- Human-caused bear deaths have the greatest affect on population growth.
- In 1975, the American grizzly was added to the federal Endangered Species List.

The Mating Game

Late spring is grizzly mating season.

Grizzly bears mate in late May or early June. A female bear will mate when she is 4 or more years old. When a female is ready to mate, a male grizzly locates her by smell. Sometimes, more than one male will locate the same female. A smaller male will leave if a larger male wants to mate with the female. If bears of equal size and strength both want to mate with the same bear, they will fight. The winning bear mates with the female.

Most of the time, grizzlies live alone. Only during mating season do the males and females come together.

Once grizzlies mate, the female's eggs fertilize, but they do not implant in her uterus right away. Instead, her body continues to prepare for hibernation. If the bear can find food and store fat, she will have as many as 3 cubs. If she has a difficult time finding food, she may not become pregnant at all. When winter approaches, a female enters her den. If she is pregnant, the cubs will be born in about 8 weeks.

Cubs

Grizzly cubs are born blind and helpless. At birth they weigh about 20 to 25 ounces (600 to 700 grams). While they are still in the den, the cubs feed on their mother's milk. Her rich milk helps them to gain weight quickly. When they come out of the den in the spring, they can follow their mother.

The first year of life is very dangerous for grizzly cubs. In fact, almost 35 percent die during this time. They rely on their mother's ability to protect them from hungry wolves and wild cats. A mother also has to find enough food for her family so her cubs do not starve. The young cubs learn the skills of self-defense and how to find food by watching their mother's behavior every day.

Left, top and bottom: A mother must work hard to provide food for her cubs and to protect them.

Young bears also learn skills by playing. A cub will play with sticks, rocks, and its brothers and sisters. While playing, cubs learn balance, coordination, and movement skills. Play also increases their strength and speed.

Bear cubs stay with their mother for 2 to 3 years. Mothers spend much of their lives raising cubs. A grizzly mother raises her cubs by herself without any help from a male. When the mother is ready to mate again, she drives the cubs off to find their own homes. They have to search for home territories with good food sources that are not already claimed by an adult bear.

Above and below: Play helps cubs to learn vital survival skills and increases strength and speed.

Bears and Humans

Less than 200 years ago, grizzly bears used to be common throughout North America. Since that time, humans have moved into many grizzly habitats. As this happened, grizzlies had less undeveloped land on which to hunt for food and raise their young. Many bears were shot because they killed and ate cattle and sheep from nearby ranches.

In 1975, the U.S. Fish and Wildlife Service declared the grizzly bear a threatened species in the lower 48 states. After careful monitoring and strict laws that protected the species, grizzlies have begun to make a small comeback in the United States.

Grizzly habitats have been steadily taken over by humans.

National Parks are a good place to see grizzly bears.

North America's National Parks are very important to the grizzly bears' survival. Vast areas of wilderness in the United States, (Yellowstone, Glacier and Denali National Park) and in Canada (Banff and Jasper National Parks) give the grizzly room to roam safely. For grizzly bears to survive, humans need to work hard to preserve these important wilderness areas.

Grizzly Bear Facts

Name: Grizzly Bear

Scientific Name: Ursus arctos

Shoulder Height: 3–3½ feet (91–107 centimeters)

Body Length: 6–7 feet (183–213 centimeters)

Weight: 325–850 pounds (147–385 kilograms)

Color: Dark brown to light brown or blond with grizzled appearance

Reaches sexual maturity: 3 years

Females mate: every 3 years

Gestation (pregnancy period): Approximately 8 months (development does not begin until the fifth month)

Litter size: 1 to 4 cubs (usual size is 2)

Social life: Lives alone; young live with mother; male and female meet at mating season

Favorite food: Whatever the bear can find

Habitat: Can be found in almost any habitat in North America where it can repeatedly find food.

Glossary

den Place where a bear will spend the winter.

extinct No longer exists anywhere on Earth, gone forever.

grizzled Gray haired.

hibernate The time when a bear goes into its den and will not eat, drink, or go to the bathroom during winter months.

home range Where the bear spends most of its time hunting for food.

For More Information

Books

Bright, Michael. *Bears and Pandas* (Nature Watch). New York, NY: Lorenz Books, 2000.

Parker, Janice. *Grizzly Bears* (Untamed World). New York, NY: Raintree/Steck-Vaughn, 2000.

Stonehouse, Bernard. Martin Camm (Illustrator). Richard Orr (Illustrator). *A Visual Introduction to Bears* (Animal Watch Series). New York, NY: Checkmark Books, 1998.

Video

Grisan: *The North American Grizzly Bear*. Stoney-Wolf Productions, Inc., 1998.

Web Site

The Bear Den

Find out facts about the different species of bears. Links to a special section for kids—

www.nature-net.com/bears

Index